Your Purpose Puzzle

Discover
Your *Why*

LifeMark Publications
2500 Dallas Parkway, Suite 495
Plano, TX 75093

ISBN: 978-0-9890230-4-7

Design by Angeline Collier / Halo Creative
www.halocreative.com

Table of Contents

We all desire purpose in our life. What were we designed to do? What will fulfill us? What difference will our life make? The mission of LifeMark Ministries is to **guide you to boldly use your God-given talents and abilities to make an eternal mark with your life — *your eMark*.** We do this by equipping you to:

- Learn more about God and know Him more intimately;
- Live a life that reflects and honors Him.

To learn more about this ministry, visit our website: **www.LifeMarkMinistries.org**

LifeMark Ministries was founded by **Mark Schupbach**, a businessman with a desire to use the experience, gifts, and talents he has been given by God to support and equip believers in their faith journey.

Mark's involvement with the church and ministry began more than 30 years ago. He has served as an elder and president on three church governing boards in both Wichita, KS, and Dallas, TX. He was involved in Bible Study Fellowship for 17 years, including serving as the Men's Teaching Leader in Dallas for 9 years. In 2003, Mark founded Next Step Bible Study to encourage participants to seek a deeper, more intimate relationship with the Lord Jesus Christ. With a firm reliance on the Holy Spirit, Mark enjoys exhorting believers to get out of their "comfort zone" and fulfill their purpose. Mark has been married to his wife, Marty, since 1969. They have 3 married daughters and 6 grandchildren.

Jennifer Hicks has a diverse background in both business and ministry, and she enjoys using her experience to encourage others in their life journey. Working with Mark since 2007, she is grateful to God for opportunities to use her gifts and skill sets in a wide variety of projects. One of her favorite things to do is spend the day behind a camera capturing the special moments of life as a freelance photographer. She also enjoys sports, especially Aggie football!

It Takes a Team!

We are so blessed to have a team of people who work together in fulfilling God's purpose for our ministry. We would like to give a special thank you to the following people for their efforts in developing this book: Angeline Collier, The Keahons, The McDougals, Elizabeth Newsome, Kathy Prather, George and Pam Reese, and Marty Schupbach. We deeply appreciate all you do!

Preface

What was the last business seminar or church conference you attended? You probably left feeling energized and excited — ready to tackle your next project. You heard lots of tips and catchy phrases to help you remember your plan and spur you on to success. Once the excitement inevitably passed and you forgot the catchy phrases, you slowly slid back into your old habits because you missed the most important question of all: **Why?**

Why does this matter? Why is this important? Why are we here? The answer to these questions provides the fuel that drives the engine of change. It is what motivates you to stick with something. To answer the "why" questions, you must have an understanding of your purpose.

Ponder your life for a moment. Why are you living in your town? Why do you have the job you have? Why are you in a specific relationship? Why are you living in your current conditions, whatever they might be? I submit to you that if you think this is all happenstance, chance, coincidence, or perhaps just accidental, you are wrong.

God has a purpose for everyone — a purpose that He determined for us before we were even born. He created us specifically for this purpose. However, we rarely see the full picture of our purpose. Rather, He reveals pieces of it over time, and our job is to assemble the puzzle and faithfully carry out our purpose. If the majority of your daily tasks are not moving you forward in this journey, you will lose momentum and find yourself drifting like a nomad. Think of your purpose as "home base." Not all of your activities will be tethered to it, but it will be your source of fuel to accomplish the things God has planned for you.

Before you start your journey, take a moment and ask God to guide you through the process of discovering your purpose. Ask the Holy Spirit to be active in this journey. We have also prayed for this process to be effective in equipping readers to fulfill their purpose.

Do not be discouraged if this journey takes time. Step by step, God will reveal His plans for you in His perfect timing. Someday, you will reflect on your **Purpose Puzzle** and be wowed with the beauty of the picture He created.

Are you ready to see what God has in store for you?

> Trust in the Lord with all your heart and lean not on your own understanding; in all your ways submit to him, and he will make your paths straight.
>
> Proverbs 3:5-6 (NIV)

Four Foundational Truths

Sounds great, but where do you start? You will discover fairly early in the process that this journey may be one of the most important exercises you have ever done. When you grasp it, the gravity of the implications may give you pause. Therefore, it is not uncommon for people to stop before they really make progress. Subconsciously, you may even have some fear about where this process may take you. Do not worry — you are not alone! It is perfectly natural to have some qualms about the future. Overcoming these fears requires you to accept that God is bigger than your circumstances. You do not need to fear the unknown because you can know the One who holds the future.

Start by asking yourself this fundamental question: **Do you trust God?** I mean, *REALLY* trust God? ...without limitations? ...in every aspect of your life? Trust is something that takes time to develop. You can probably reflect on times in your life where God was there for you, demonstrating His trustworthiness. Even though these experiences have molded us to accept His trustworthiness intellectually and emotionally, it can still be difficult to trust Him with our future. *However, trusting Him is essential to pursuing your purpose.*

Before you begin working on your **Purpose Puzzle**, let us examine four foundational truths that will facilitate the trust-building process. Most people begin a puzzle by separating the edge pieces from the inside pieces and assembling the frame of the puzzle. This frame creates a glimpse of what the end product will look like without giving away the picture itself.

In a similar way, these four foundational truths will be the frame of your **Purpose Puzzle**. They will keep you from getting off-track as you seek His will for your life.

Truth #1:
You were made *ON purpose and FOR a purpose.*

God created you intentionally. He formed you in your mother's womb and created your inmost being (Psalms 139:13). If you have ever studied how a baby grows in its mother's womb, you know how incredibly intricate the process is and how important the timing is. That type of development can only be explained by the all-knowing God who created you.

You are not here by accident. God designed you to fulfill His plans for your life. "My frame was not hidden from you when I was made in the secret place, when I was woven together in the depths of the earth. Your eyes saw my unformed body; all the days ordained for me were written in your book before one of them came to be" (Psalm 139:15-16, NIV).

Imagine that! God knew every day of your life before you were even born. He knew you would be reading this book today, seeking His will for your life.

Believing that you were created **ON purpose and FOR a purpose** is foundational to moving forward – it provides the base edge for your Purpose Puzzle.

> For we are his workmanship, having been created in Christ Jesus for good works that God prepared beforehand so we may do them.
>
> Ephesians 2:10 (NET)

Truth #1: ON purpose & FOR a purpose

Truth #2:
Seek FIRST His Kingdom, and everything else will fall into place.

Where is your focus? What consumes your thoughts, your time, and your resources? Do you find yourself worrying about your family, job, finances, or future? Does your desire to live in a nice home or drive an expensive car cause you to feel anxious about making enough money to meet your obligations?

> But above all pursue his kingdom and righteousness, and all these things will be given to you as well.
>
> Matthew 6:33 (NET)

Do not misunderstand — there is nothing wrong with enjoying nice things in life. However, it is imperative to guard against making "things" into a god and allowing them to determine your life choices. *Set your focus on God and His purpose for your life.* He will take care of all the other things when you seek Him first.

Realize, that does not mean that you will get every material thing your heart desires! It does mean that He will meet your needs and that in seeking His Kingdom ahead of your own, you will find that your personal desires gradually grow more in line with His plans. It is a faith journey, one step at a time.

One way you can seek His Kingdom is to read the Bible daily. Psalm 119:105 tells us that God's Word will be the lamp that illuminates our path. Imagine walking in a park at night and having the option of a path that is well-lit and one that is dark — which one would you choose? By regularly reading the Bible, we keep that light shining brightly in our lives. This equips us to stay on His path for our lives as we seek His Kingdom above everything else.

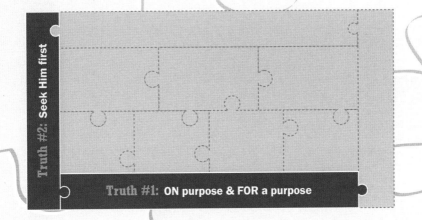

Truth #2: Seek Him first

Truth #1: ON purpose & FOR a purpose

Truth #3:

Living life this way fills us with a deep joy and a supernatural peace – the kind of peace that passes all understanding.

What keeps you awake at night? What stresses weigh you down? What robs you of peace and joy? Society tries to convince you that the answers to life's problems can be found through relationships, money, shopping, food, sex, drugs, popularity — you name it. The message that you are your own source of peace and happiness is often proclaimed by Hollywood celebrities and heard on the news. The culture is seeking what **only God can give because He is the true source of deep joy and peace.**

If you do not believe me, pay attention to television ads. What themes do you see? What people are most idealized? We are off track! Even though most people acknowledge their emptiness, they do not change because either they do not want to or they do not know how to.

At some point, many of us discover that only God can fill the hole in our lives, and we fall to our knees in dependence on Him. My prayer for you is that it does not take a disaster or tragedy to get you to that point. The fact that you are reading this book shows you are already keenly aware of this and are seeking your purpose...*one that will matter for eternity.* Once you know your purpose, you can pursue it whole-heartedly and experience joy and peace like never before.

> You lead me in the path of life; I experience absolute joy in your presence; you always give me sheer delight.
>
> Psalm 16:11 (NET)

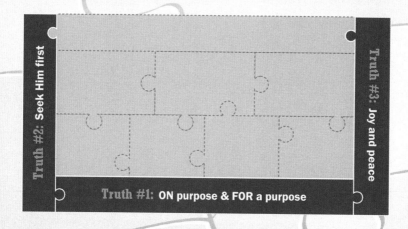

Truth #2: Seek Him first

Truth #3: Joy and peace

Truth #1: ON purpose & FOR a purpose

Truth #4:

When we seek and fulfill His purpose for our lives, we will someday hear, *"Well done, good and faithful servant."*

While our actions should overflow as a reflection of our love for God, it is also motivating to know that someday we will be rewarded in heaven for the things we do. Did you know that? In 1 Corinthians 4, Paul told his audience of believers that when the Lord returns, He will *"bring to light what is hidden in darkness and will expose the motives of the heart" (NIV).* Paul continues, *"At that time each will receive their praise from God."*

Let's face it, living this way is not easy because it runs counter to the world. It starts with belief — not deeds, works, or wishes...*just belief.* Many people find that difficult because we are raised to believe that nothing is free and that we must work to earn everything. However, God's gift of salvation is completely free! Next, it requires faith because your beliefs will be challenged daily. This faith will help you develop total trust in God which you will need because fulfilling your purpose is an act of continuous, daily obedience. This sounds difficult, but do not grow discouraged because God will give you strength to do it.

> His master replied, 'Well done, good and faithful servant! You have been faithful with a few things; I will put you in charge of many things. Come and share your master's happiness!'
>
> Matthew 25:21 (NIV)

As you seek your God-given purpose, press on with the desire that when you meet the Lord face-to-face, you will hear, *"Well done, good and faithful servant. I put you there for this purpose, and you did it obediently. Well done."*

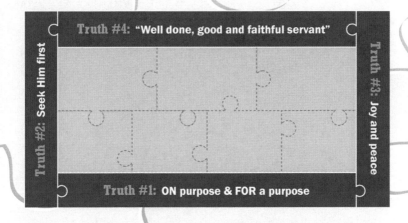

Truth #4: "Well done, good and faithful servant"

Truth #2: Seek Him first

Truth #3: Joy and peace

Truth #1: ON purpose & FOR a purpose

Now what?

Now that you have the frame of your Purpose Puzzle in place, it is time to address the inside pieces. Ask God to reveal His purpose for you as you work your way through the 7 P's of Purpose. This will be an exciting, though sometimes difficult, journey of discovery. Keep trusting in Him each step of the way, and press on!

Piecing It All Together:
7 P's of Purpose

You have a responsibility to discover your purpose. It is important to realize that even though it is *your purpose*, it is not for *your benefit* — **it is for the benefit of others**. It is not about you! Your purpose, by the power of the Holy Spirit in you and through you, is to love God and serve others.

While there is no formula for finding your purpose, there are things you can do to assist in the discovery process. This next section will walk you through these steps. All seven are important, but they may not be of equal importance at this point in your life. Although each of the seven can be independent from one another, it is interesting how God weaves them together in a beautiful and supernatural way — pointing you to His purpose for you.

If you are reading this book digitally, you will want to take two sheets of paper and divide each sheet into 4 boxes like the example on the next page. Keep these papers nearby so you can take notes as you progress through the 7 P's of Purpose on the pages that follow. For each P, there will be an application box at the bottom of the page with questions to help you think through your personal application.

Toward the back of this book, you will see a few examples of completed puzzles. If you do not understand one of the categories or are having difficulty answering some of the questions, review these examples. You might find them helpful as you go through the process yourself.

Sheet 1:

Prayer	Past
Profession	**Position**

Sheet 2:

People	Priorities
Passion	***PURPOSE***

The 7 P's of Purpose

1: Prayer

Everything starts with prayer. The most important part of prayer is not *speaking* — it is *listening*. Start with something like, *"God, please help me see Your purpose for my life."* Then, listen. God will use the Holy Spirit in you to guide you as you seek Him in prayer. You will also need to commit to praying over each step of the discovery process. Use prayer to seek continual reinforcement of what you believe God is showing you.

Because God's purpose for you will typically be bigger than you can imagine, you will probably get to a point where you think, *"I think this is what my purpose is...*gulp*...but I'm not sure."* God calls you to step forward — just take a step in the direction you believe He is calling you. Then, after seeking more direction, take another step...and another one. With each step, your continual prayer is, *"God, am I on the right path? Please help me to stay on Your path for my life."*

> Ask and it will be given to you; seek and you will find; knock and the door will be opened to you. For everyone who asks receives; the one who seeks finds; and to the one who knocks, the door will be opened.
>
> Matthew 7:7-8 (NIV)

God will be faithful to reveal His purpose for you as you seek Him. Psalm 5:3 reminds you to wait expectantly and patiently after you have submitted your prayers to God. Sometimes He will confirm you are on His path. Other times, He will block your path — do not get discouraged when this happens. God guides by both opening and closing doors. Sometimes, we wait awhile for answers, but even in times of silence, God is at work.

Daniel was a faithful prayer warrior, even in the face of persecution. He knew that following God's plan might cost him his life, but he also knew that **the God he served was bigger than the enemy he faced**. Prayer is our lifeline to God, and you will need to rely on it throughout this discovery process.

Puzzle Piece Discovery

Before you move forward, write down a prayer asking God to reveal His purpose for you as you work your way through the remaining 6 P's of Purpose. With each P, spend some quiet, uninterrupted time praying and listening.

Your Prayer "Puzzle Piece" Notes

_____

_____

_____

_____

_____

_____

_____

_____

_____

_____

_____

_____

_____

_____

_____

_____

_____

_____

_____

_____

_____

_____

_____

_____

Mark's Musings

- This step cannot be overemphasized!

- Plug into the power that is available to you through the Holy Spirit.

- Be patient and allow Him to gradually reveal the picture to you.

2: Past

You may be thinking, *"But, I have spent years trying to forget my past!"* However, there is so much benefit in reviewing your past and learning from it. Many past experiences fall into one of three categories:

1. **The Good:** Doing the right thing, the right way, at the right time, and getting good results.
2. **The Bad:** Doing the wrong thing and getting bad results.
3. **The Ugly:** Things that just happen...not as a result of anything you did or did not do.

Let your past *prepare you*, but do not let it *control you*. Consider Peter's example. He witnessed the transfiguration (Matthew 17) and walked on water to meet Jesus (Matthew 14). However, he also started to sink in the water because of his fear. He even denied knowing Jesus three times, something he could not imagine doing. Yet, Jesus told him that once he turned back and was restored, He wanted Peter to strengthen his brothers.

> Because of the Lord's great love we are not consumed, for his compassions never fail. They are new every morning; great is your faithfulness. I say to myself, 'The Lord is my portion; therefore I will wait for him.'
>
> Lamentations 3:22-24 (NIV)

Peter was not held captive by his past (good, bad, or ugly). After Jesus' resurrection, He made sure that Peter was fully restored and called on Peter to feed the Church. God loves us so much that He sets us free from our past, but it still has an influence on the person we have become and how He will use us.

You can benefit from *all* your life experiences. Others can benefit from your experiences as well. Your past gives you the authority to talk about things you have personally experienced. Sometimes, you need to remind yourself what those things are.

Puzzle Piece Discovery

Write down some of your past experiences (good, bad, and ugly). Beside each one, write down some of the ways you grew from these experiences. Ask God to use your past to prepare you for His future for you so that others may benefit from your counsel.

Your Past "Puzzle Piece" Notes

_____

_____

_____

_____

_____

_____

_____

_____

_____

_____

_____

_____

_____

_____

_____

_____

_____

_____

_____

_____

_____

_____

_____

_____

_____

_____

Mark's Musings

- I tend to want to rush through this step because I have tried hard to forget some of my past! However, this is such a vital step, so take time to reflect on your past — the good, bad, and even the ugly!

- Many things of value are formed in the midst of ugliness (for example, diamonds and pearls). Allow the dark parts of your past to shape you into the person He created you to be!

3: Profession

Beyond your job title, what are your skills, talents, and abilities? In what areas do you have expertise? What do you do better than others? In what areas do you have the experience to authoritatively talk to other people?

You have at least one or two areas — most likely, you have a lot of them. Competencies can be in a variety of areas. The following list is not comprehensive, but it will help you think through some possibilities.

Technical: craftsmanship, engineering, designing, building, repairing
Process: organizing, implementing, budgeting, solving problems
Creative: decorating, writing, speaking, generating ideas, storytelling, cooking
Relational: empathizing, listening, coaching, counseling, serving, motivating others, communicating

> There are different kinds of gifts, but the same Spirit distributes them. There are different kinds of service, but the same Lord. There are different kinds of working, but in all of them and in everyone it is the same God at work.
>
> 1 Corinthians 12:4-6 (NIV)

Typically, these strengths come so naturally to you that you might not think they are special. A lack of awareness or confidence may prevent you from fully utilizing your skills. Be careful that you do not diminish your abilities. Learn to use them for the benefit of others in order to fulfill God's purpose in your life. Nehemiah was a great example of organizing the people to use their skill sets in order to accomplish amazing things in a short period of time.

In addition, as a believer, you have one or more **spiritual gifts** that further enhance your skills and equip you supernaturally to accomplish God's will. You can read more about these gifts in Romans 12:3-8, 1 Corinthians 12, and Ephesians 4:11-16. There are also many tests available to help you discover your spiritual gifts.

Puzzle Piece Discovery

Write down three things you do really well and enjoy doing. Also, ask five friends to tell you three strengths or skills at which you excel. Combine their lists and compare them with yours — what recurring skills do you see? What has been successful? In addition, take a Spiritual Gifts test, and write down your results. Where do your skills and gifts overlap?

Your Profession "Puzzle Piece" Notes

_____

_____

_____

_____

_____

_____

_____

_____

_____

_____

_____

_____

_____

_____

_____

_____

_____

_____

_____

_____

_____

_____

_____

_____

Mark's Musings

- Come on now...don't be shy! I bet there are at least a couple of things you do really well.

- Use your imagination to think outside the box!

- This one might surprise you — what you do really well might not have much to do with your actual occupation.

4: Position

Consider your current position in life. Whether it is your job, geographic location, or status, you have a unique position that God has designed to help you fulfill His purpose in and through you. Perhaps you are an excellent networker and can connect needs to people who are equipped to meet those needs. Maybe you are in a financial position to meet the needs God puts in your view.

It is very important to note that you do not have to be rich or well-connected to have a position. It is possible that your position as a mother of young children opens the door for you to be an encourager to other mothers. As a school janitor, you might see children who are struggling when no one else is looking. As an employee at a call center, you talk to hundreds of people with whom you would never connect otherwise.

> As for you, you meant to harm me, but God intended it for a good purpose, so he could preserve the lives of many people, as you can see this day.
>
> Genesis 50:20 (NET)

In Genesis, we see God place Joseph in a variety of positions as He equipped him to prepare Egypt and Israel for a coming famine. Joseph was sold into slavery by his own brothers. In Egypt, he eventually served Potiphar, the captain of Pharaoh's guard. However, Potiphar's wife lied about Joseph, and Potiphar had him put in prison. His God-given gift for interpreting dreams eventually brought him before Pharaoh who had experienced dreams that no one had been able to interpret. However, God gave Joseph the ability to understand Pharaoh's dreams, and thus he was promoted to be in charge of the palace and **all** of Pharaoh's holdings. He told Joseph, "only with respect to the throne will I be greater than you."

Imagine what Joseph must have been thinking as his positions changed. He went from being the favorite son of his father to being a slave, then to controlling all of Potiphar's household to being jailed unjustly, and eventually to becoming second in power of all of Egypt! Even though Joseph's circumstances were often difficult, they were crucial in preparing him to fulfill God's purpose in his life.

Puzzle Piece Discovery

Write down your current position — your job, status, geographic location, connections, financial position, etc. Acknowledge that God has placed you in this position for a reason, and ask Him to reveal His purpose for your current position. Write down any thoughts that come to mind as you listen for His response.

Your Position "Puzzle Piece" Notes

_____
_____
_____
_____
_____
_____
_____
_____
_____
_____
_____
_____
_____
_____
_____
_____
_____
_____
_____
_____
_____
_____
_____
_____
_____
_____
_____
_____
_____
_____
_____

Mark's Musings

- If you are struggling with this one, consider who you influence.

- Who listens when you talk?

- Do you find this part challenging? Well, congratulations — you are normal!

5: People

This puzzle piece actually has two components: 1) the people in need and 2) the people with whom you can partner. Let's take a closer look at each category.

While most people like to claim that they love everyone, the reality is that you cannot meet everyone's needs. **You have been uniquely focused by God's Spirit to see a specific group of people as He sees them — to have a deep desire to help them, to care for them, to meet their needs, and to introduce them to Jesus.** Whether it is inner-city youth, unwed mothers, widows, orphans, business leaders, your church youth group, or people living in third-world countries, you likely have a special tenderness toward a specific group of people. You will be able to better understand their needs and relate to them because God has equipped you to do so through the Holy Spirit.

Who shares your love for this group? How can you connect with others to accomplish His purpose through you? In the Bible, God often brought people together for a mission. In Luke 10, Jesus appointed some of His followers and sent them out in pairs to prepare the people ahead of Him.

Paul also strongly encouraged working with other believers in pursuing God's purpose. At the end of 1 Corinthians, Paul urged the church to submit to those doing the work of the Lord. He shares of his joy in having believers come alongside and refresh his spirit. Who refreshes your spirit? Consider partnering with them in doing the Lord's work.

> Two people are better than one, because they can reap more benefit from their labor. For if they fall, one will help his companion up, but pity the person who falls down and has no one to help him up. Furthermore, if two lie down together, they can keep each other warm, but how can one person keep warm by himself? Although an assailant may overpower one person, two can withstand him. Moreover, a three-stranded cord is not quickly broken.
>
> Ecclesiastes 4:9-12 (NET)

Puzzle Piece Discovery

Divide your people box in half. On the left side, describe the people you tend to have a special tenderness toward. On the right side, write down the names of five people with whom you would like to partner to pursue helping meet the needs God is enabling you to see.

Your People "Puzzle Piece" Notes

_____
_____
_____
_____
_____
_____
_____
_____
_____
_____
_____
_____
_____
_____
_____
_____
_____
_____
_____
_____
_____
_____
_____
_____
_____
_____
_____
_____
_____

Mark's Musings

- Do not try to accomplish your purpose alone — partner with people of like mind.

- Allow the Holy Spirit to leverage you with others in order to accomplish amazing things for God's glory.

6: Priorities

As Dr. Howard Hendricks once said, *"You are able to do many things, but be sure you find the one thing you must do."* **Your top priority in life is the one thing you cannot *not do.***

Imagine yourself taking a trip in your car. As you drive along, you see things through your windshield — warning signs, people, other cars, exit ramps, etc. In a similar fashion, consider your life as a car trip. What or who keeps reappearing in your windshield? Everywhere you look, you see a specific need: it is on the news, in a ministry support letter, in an email forwarded by a friend. Perhaps it is something in your personal life such as a disease that has affected a loved one or a problem that has caused a rift in your family. You care about it so deeply that you are likely either making it a priority or you are feeling guilty that you have not yet done so.

Perhaps you find yourself desiring to make something a priority because your heart is in it, but you have trouble following through. **Often, you have to stop doing things in areas that you determine are not high priorities in order to allow time to do the things that matter most to you.** Everyone has "idols" in their lives — money, power, influence, affluence, etc. If you notice one of these becoming the top priority in your life, ask God to help you refocus on Him. Priorities can easily and quickly shift in a direction that is unintentional. You end up *reacting* to situations rather than *intentionally pursuing* the things about which you care most. The exercise below will help you evaluate your situation and make the changes you desire.

> No one can serve two masters. Either you will hate the one and love the other, or you will be devoted to the one and despise the other. You cannot serve both God and money.
>
> Matthew 6:24 (NIV)

It is important to continue to pray as you seek clarity determining your priorities. Later in this book, we will talk more in depth about how you can know if your priorities are in order and when you are on the right track.

Puzzle Piece Discovery

On a separate sheet of paper (not your form), write down the current ways you are spending your time and resources. Do they match the priorities God wants you to have? If not, what changes can you make? Write these changes down on your form and consider asking a friend to hold you accountable to implement them.

Your Priorities "Puzzle Piece" Notes

_____
_____
_____
_____
_____
_____
_____
_____
_____
_____
_____
_____
_____
_____
_____
_____
_____
_____
_____
_____
_____
_____
_____
_____
_____
_____
_____
_____
_____
_____

Mark's Musings

- Learning to say "no" is very difficult for most people. However, if you are going to accomplish His will in your life, you need to learn!

- Do you feel bad when you say "no" to someone? Focus on the things you can accomplish because you have said no to distractions.

- Try smiling when you say no — it will make it easier!

7: Passion

When you hear the word "passion", you probably connect it with an emotional feeling. However, passion about your purpose is something so deeply ingrained that it drives you. Always close to the surface, it is what dominates your mind when you are not thinking about anything. It is what overflows when you are talking with your family or friends about what is going on in your life. Sometimes, you can get so passionate about something that you end up preaching to whoever will listen, even if it is the guy on the elevator whom you have just met.

Spirit-inspired passion fuels the engine of purpose. It will keep you moving forward when you are too tired to continue. It will encourage you to sacrifice your time, talents, and resources in a way that is supernatural and unexplainable to the outside world. It is the Holy Spirit in you, reminding you that the needs you see matter and that He will empower you to do something about them.

> Therefore, I urge you, brothers and sisters, in view of God's mercy, to offer your bodies as a living sacrifice, holy and pleasing to God — this is your true and proper worship.
>
> Romans 12:1 (NIV)

David was a man of passion. He devoted himself whole-heartedly as a warrior, a king, and unfortunately, as an adulterer and murderer. Despite David's humanity, God considered him "a man after God's own heart." God used David's passion to accomplish great things.

It is important to note that passion can also lead you down the wrong path, like it did for David. That is why it is imperative to stay in God's Word each day and remain grounded in His Truth. Paul reinforced this when he said, *"Do not conform to the pattern of this world, but be transformed by the renewing of your mind. Then you will be able to test and approve what God's will is — his good, pleasing and perfect will" (Romans 12:2, NIV).* You renew your mind through prayer and reading the Bible so that you are able to discern and obey God's will.

Puzzle Piece Discovery

Write down 3-5 things you feel passionate about. Keep in mind that they do not all have to be spiritual. For example, you might have a passion for feeding the hungry or for changing the direction of the country. Do not confuse passion with interest. God-given passion is much more...it is a driving force.

Your Passion "Puzzle Piece" Notes

Mark's Musings

- What fuels the fire in you?

- If you don't feel a fire toward a cause, you are probably not in your "sweet spot."

- Your passion is not about temporary things (like being a fanatical sports fan). Passion runs deep in meaning and purpose, and when applied, it benefits others.

What is Next?

Now that you have spent some time evaluating the different components to discover your purpose, take a moment to review your chart. What themes appear in more than one of your boxes? Write down your thoughts in the last box labeled "Purpose," and spend some time in prayer. Ask God to confirm or redirect what you believe you see as His purpose for you. As mentioned previously, prayer is a crucial and ongoing component to staying on God's path for your life.

Then, take a step in that direction. This could include discussing your purpose with a friend, developing a plan of implementation, learning a new skill to better prepare yourself, connecting with influential people who share your passion for your purpose, or any number of things. The important thing is to step forward in faith, asking God to confirm His will.

A Few Words of Caution

How can you know if what you are doing is God's purpose in and through you? It is easy to be consumed in the pursuit of something. Sometimes it is for noble reasons (for example, love), and sometimes it is not (for example, greed).

Typically, your purpose will be **something that God has brought into your life, not something you sought on your own.** Purpose is often revealed gradually and quietly. If you find yourself being drawn to a need and you keep seeing opportunities in your "windshield of life" to meet the need, then take steps in that direction. As you act, continually talk with the Lord and ask Him to confirm that you are following His lead. Take a step and pray, *"God, if this is from You, bless it and open the doors ahead. If it is not from You, keep me out of it! I do not want to be where You do not want me to be."*

It is important that the process of discovering your purpose is not the result of a formula. Life is not formulaic, and you must rely on a close relationship with the Lord in order to know His calling and follow His leading. One purpose may have different stages and phases. Sometimes you cannot do the ultimate purpose because you have not yet completed the earlier, smaller purposes that God has planned in order to prepare you. Other times, you are in a time of rest and preparation or a time of transition. Occasionally, you are in a phase of waiting as God orchestrates and organizes the pieces of your purpose before He places you in it. No matter what phase of life in which you find yourself, ask God to use your circumstances for His purpose in your life.

Three Proofs

Here are three proofs to watch for as you pursue your purpose — these are ways God often confirms that you are on the right track:

1. **When you do it, you get an incredible surge of energy.** It fires you up. Think of all the things in your daily life that can be energy drainers: paying bills, home maintenance, managing people, creating, cooking, decorating, speaking, writing, communicating, etc. You likely dread some of these tasks and find yourself pushing them to the bottom of the list. Carrying out your purpose is the exact opposite. It energizes you so much that when you finish doing it, you want to do it again!

2. **You may see spiritual fruit as a result of your work.** The fruit will look different, depending on the group of people you are reaching. Whether your work results in people trusting in Jesus for the first time or in people growing deeper and more mature in their faith, spiritual fruit can be a confirmation that you are right where God wants you. Having said that, it is important to recognize that sometimes the fruit does not appear initially. In fact, it is possible that you will never see the fruit of your labor. For example, Jim Elliot died at age 29, trying to reach a remote group of savages in Ecuador with the Gospel. He gave his life in pursuit of God's purpose, never seeing the fruit that would eventually come from his sacrifice. What an amazing thought that he now resides in Heaven with some of the very people who took his life and later became Christians! Together they worship at the throne of God!

3. **You have inner peace.** When you are fulfilling God's will for your life, you do not do it for public acclaim, but rather for the Lord's acclaim. He will fill you with His supernatural peace because you are doing exactly what He wants you to do.

The Difficult Road

If you have inner peace, see spiritual fruit, and get an energy gain, then you are probably fulfilling God's purpose for you! However, this does not mean that you are not going to have problems or challenges. **Even in the center of His perfect will for you, there will be difficulties and heartache...times when you have to persevere.** The beauty of it is that God will walk through the fire with you.

Jesus is our perfect example. He was fulfilling God's calling in His life to pay for our sins. His purpose was an incredibly difficult burden, and He pleaded with God to change it if there was any other way. However, Jesus humbly accepted His purpose with a desire to fulfill God's will for His life over His own will. God gave Him the strength to make the ultimate sacrifice for our sins. He gave us life through the death of His Son.

> Not only this, but we also rejoice in sufferings, knowing that suffering produces endurance, and endurance, character, and character, hope. And hope does not disappoint, because the love of God has been poured out in our hearts through the Holy Spirit who was given to us.
>
> Romans 5:3-4 (NET)

God will use the difficult times to mold you in ways you cannot imagine, preparing you for the future that only He knows. Corrie Ten Boom once commented, *"Every experience God gives us, every person He puts in our lives, is the perfect preparation for a future that only He can see."* Take courage knowing that there is a reason behind your struggles, and find comfort in sharing in Christ's sufferings.

The "Why" of Your Life

Without purpose, you will go through life doing whatever it is that you want to do, but it will leave you feeling empty and unfulfilled. As mentioned at the beginning of this book, God has a purpose for everyone — a purpose that He determined before you were even born. Your job, as you go through life, is to find it and faithfully live it.

So, you might ask, *"What is the **why** behind my purpose?"* If you are a believer, then *the purpose for your purpose is the person of Jesus Christ.* He is the reason why you do what you do. Because He first loved you and died on the cross so that you could live eternally in Heaven, you live your life desiring to share that love with others. If you are not a believer, the rest of life will likely be fun, interesting, and sometimes challenging, but it will not be purposeful or meaningful. Only Jesus is the real source of meaning in life.

Life is so short. No one knows what lies ahead. If you are not sure of what you believe about Jesus, do not let this day get away. The Bible says that everyone is a sinner and that the penalty for sin is death (Romans 3:23 and Romans 6:23). No one has lived a perfect life. We have all lied at one time or committed any number of sins, and those sins prevent us from standing in the presence of a holy and perfect God. Instead, unforgiven sinners will spend eternity separated from Him.

The wonderful news is that God loved us so much that He sent His only Son, Jesus Christ, to pay the penalty for our sins. He died on the cross and rose from the grave, overcoming death. By believing in Him and accepting God's offer of forgiveness for our sins, we can have eternal life in Heaven (John 3:16 and Romans 5:8). Forgiveness is something we will never be able to earn (Ephesians 2:8-9). **We cannot do enough good works to make up for the sins we have committed. We must simply trust in Jesus and accept His payment for our sins.**

If you would like to trust in Jesus as your Savior, just talk with God about it. That is all prayer is — a conversation between you and God. It is also important to tell someone who can help you take the next steps in your faith journey (a friend, family member, or a pastor). If you would like to learn more about this, we have some resources on our website to answer your questions and to guide you.

Most importantly, do not delay the most important decision you will make in your life. **Do not go to bed tonight until you have wrestled with this. We are not promised tomorrow.**

Conclusion

On the following pages, you will see a few examples of results from the **Your Purpose Puzzle** journey of discovery. As mentioned at the start of this book, you might find these examples helpful as you go through the process yourself.

When you are living your purpose, there is such an incredible satisfaction and joy beyond your grandest dreams. This is because:

God has enabled you,
allowed you,
gifted you,
positioned you,
and purposed you
for this time,
in this place,
to be His person
and use your life
to glorify Him and
love and serve others.

That is our prayer for you!

We would love to hear from you. Please send us your feedback, suggestions, and stories of your faith journey. You can email them to: info@lifemarkministries.org

Would you like to receive our free devotionals in your email inbox? We typically send 1-2 each week to encourage you in your faith journey. Visit our website to begin receiving them today:

www.LifeMarkMinistries.org

Sample Purpose Puzzle #1: 45-year old female

Prayer

Heavenly Father, I marvel at the knowledge that You created me for a purpose. You WANT to use me! How wonderful is that? Guide me through this process as I seek Your purpose in my life, and give me the strength to carry it out. Thank You!

Past

- Grew up as a single child in a wonderful home.
- Learned about Jesus and committed my life to Him at an early age.
- Had a happy childhood and was active in my youth group.
- Worked as a babysitter throughout my teen years.

Profession

- Good at serving others behind the scene.
- Relate well to children, and have become a mentor figure to my children's friends.
- Good communicator in person and in print.

Position

- Wife of 17 years
- Mother to 4 children ranging from age 7 to age 14
- Team mom
- Active in PTA
- Lead a Mom's group in my neighborhood

People

- I have a heart to exhort moms to be the women God has called us to be. If I can influence them for Christ, then they will influence their households for Him — and so on!
- My pastor's wife, my mother, and my next-door neighbor share this desire with me.

Priorities

- Be active in my children's lives — listening and supporting; correcting when necessary, and most importantly, cultivating a love for Jesus in their hearts.
- Support my husband as he leads the family
- Equip and encourage other moms

Passion

- God has given mothers such an important role, but our society often degrades the role and attempts to tell us that motherhood is not valuable.
- Children cannot raise themselves. We are to lovingly steward them as gifts from God and point them toward Him.

PURPOSE

My purpose is to cultivate a home environment that is honoring to the Lord and to guide other women to do the same. I am called to exemplify Jesus to my family through my actions and words, and build into my children, especially while they are living at home.

Sample Purpose Puzzle #2: 30-year old male

Prayer God, I know You have a reason for my life. You saved me from myself and from the destructive path I was walking. I want to accomplish Your purpose through me — help me discover that purpose as I seek You in each step of this journey.	**Past** - Grew up in the inner city. - Got trapped in a lifestyle of gangs, drugs, sex, and alcohol. - My grandmother influenced me; I knew she was different from others, but I didn't make it personal in my life. - Found Jesus while in prison.
Profession - Sales job - Telling stories - Playing basketball - Reaching the lost where they are - General business skills	**Position** - Living in the projects as an outreach. - Single male; no family or responsibility. - Flexible schedule due to sales job.
People - Inner-city boys and young men are my target audience. - Others who also see this need would be my cousin, my pastor, and the basketball coach at the local high school.	**Priorities** - Earn a modest income in a part-time role that allows me to have time to "be there" for these guys. - Hang out at the schools, build relationships with the counselors, coaches, and teachers. - Be a father figure for boys who need one.
Passion - Help young inner-city boys avoid the traps I fell into. - Transform my neighborhood for Jesus!	**PURPOSE** To display the love of Jesus to young boys living in the inner city through the use of my past experiences and my basketball and life skills; to teach them about God the Father by being a father figure to those who don't have one.

Sample Purpose Puzzle #3: 60-year old male

Prayer

God, I know You have purpose for my life beyond the mundane daily tasks. Help me to discover why You made me and carry out Your purpose in me. I don't want to get to the end of my life and regret how I spent it. I want to do the things You have prepared for me to do.

Past

- Business successes and failures.
- Founded and sold a successful internet company early in my career, providing flexibility in my future.
- Divorced mid-life after an affair; biggest regret in my life

Profession

- Have my MBA.
- Excellent at identifying skills and strengths in others and organizing a team to accomplish big things.
- Good at developing creative solutions for problems in life & business.
- Good networker.

Position

- CEO of a company I founded 10 years ago; I have a flexible schedule that will allow me to pursue other interests.
- Divorced; father of 3 grown sons.
- Participant in an organization geared toward helping business leaders.

People

- I have a desire to help mid-life, male business leaders who get stuck in a rut — I want them to see there is more to life before it is too late.
- My former colleague and my roommate from college both share this desire to help these men.

Priorities

- Growing my business
- Developing an "exit strategy"
- Coaching male business leaders
- Coaching middle-aged men to re-engage in life and find their purpose so they don't fall prey to bad distractions

Passion

- I want to help other men avoid the pitfalls I fell into: pride, believing I was untouchable, greed, and pornography. These things destroyed the life I had so meticulously built, and now that I have repented before the Lord, He has restored me and equipped me to help other men.

PURPOSE

I believe my purpose is to help middle-aged men discover their purpose and encourage them to pursue what God desires for them.

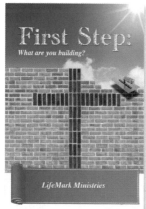

First Step: Laying the Foundation for a God-honoring Life

In any building project, the most critical stage is laying a solid foundation. It is the same for our Christianity, too. If we know the basics of our faith, then we will be able to weather the storms of life.

This 10-week study is designed to ground you in those basics. Whether you are a new believer or someone who has been a Christian for years but wants to review the foundations of your faith, you will find this study to be helpful. The following five topics are covered, with two weeks on each topic: God the Father, The Bible, God the Son, God the Holy Spirit, and The Holy Trinity. For each topic, there will be verses to read, questions to answer, and a summary of the video. The videos are available separately as part of the First Step Leader's Kit.

Aging with Honor: A Practical Guide to Help You Honor Your Parents as They Age

Growing up is hard to do. That's why God gave kids parents — to teach, train, help, and guide them as they go from having a lot of limitations to having a lot of freedoms and into adulthood.

Growing old is even harder. That's why God gave parents kids — to encourage, support, help, and guide them as they go from having a lot of freedoms to having a lot of limitations.

This practical guide will cover a variety of issues in five individual segments: Financial Needs, Medical Needs, Logistical Needs, Relational Needs, and Spiritual Needs. It will provide you with the tools and resources that you will need in order to evaluate your situation and create a plan that works best for your family.

Mark is also available for speaking engagements and conferences. To find out more, visit our website:

www.LifeMarkMinistries.org

Mosaic of the Master

Jesus was born. He served. He died and was resurrected.

We all know the basics of the greatest story in history. Most of us have heard the details for years. We celebrate at Christmas and Easter every year, and we often quote famous passages from the Bible.

However, those basics are simply vital pieces in the mosaic of Who Jesus is. The four Gospel authors give a much more in-depth and thorough picture of Jesus — His teachings, His miracles, His submission to the Father, His love and compassion for the least among us, His very heart.

Each piece will show you a different aspect of Jesus through the eyes of Matthew, Mark, Luke, and John. You will be challenged to grow in new ways as you piece together Jesus' story and see the beautiful mosaic God painted of His Son through His Word. *It will change your own life story!*

Volume 1: This 27-week study through the first half of the four Gospels simultaneously will help you draw closer than ever before to your Savior as you journey alongside Him as a boy and into manhood, watching Him teach in the temple, heal the sick, feed the hungry, show mercy to sinners, raise the dead, challenge hypocrites, and more.

Volume 2: This 27-week study through the second half of the four Gospels will grow your faith as you observe Jesus continuing to minister to sinners and preparing to die for our sins. You will weep with Peter as he denies Christ, celebrate with the women as they find the tomb empty, and marvel with the many witnesses who saw Jesus after the resurrection.

Each book includes assigned reading and questions to help you dive into God's Word. On our website, you will find the videos of "The Talk" given each week to reinforce what you have studied. You can do this study on your own, but we encourage you to assemble a small group and glean insight from one another as you progress through the study.

To find out more about these and other resources, to sign up to receive our free devotional emails, or to place an order, visit our website:

www.LifeMarkMinistries.org

Made in the USA
Monee, IL
02 August 2021